CREDIBILITY METHOD

THE SIMPLE METHOD TO ESTABLISHING YOUR CREDIBILITY & INCREASING YOUR LEGITIMACY IN YOUR INDUSTRY OR CAREER.

BY MYKE METZGER

www.mykemetzger.com

Table of Contents

It would be a real shame if you end up being a statistical probability that opens this book and never finishes it. What you're about to read (**IF** you read it) will drastically transform your momentum as a business owner, real estate agent, influencer, entrepreneur, speaker, or really just about anything.

I don't believe in "getting rich quick". I believe in hard and consistent work, building intelligent leverage, adding value to the world we live in, and serving others with my expertise. That's what this book is designed to help you do as well. I can not and do not make any guarantees about your own ability to get results or earn any money with my ideas, information, books, strategies, or programs. I most likely don't know you - and besides, your results in life are entirely up to you. I'm simply here to help by giving you my greatest strategies to move you forward, faster.

Throughout this book I will mention a lot of resources, strategies, and tools that will be marked with this star - ★. When you see that star at anytime, you can access the related information at **www.credibilitymethod.com/free**

I don't care what circumstances you come from, if you apply what you learn in this book it will work for you. So please be an exception to the rule, and be the one who stands out, reads, implements and succeeds.

To all of your future success,

- Myke

www.credibilitymethod.com/amazon

If you finish and enjoy this book, as well as the free resources
that have been provided for you, it would mean the world to me
if you left a review of the book with your feedback.

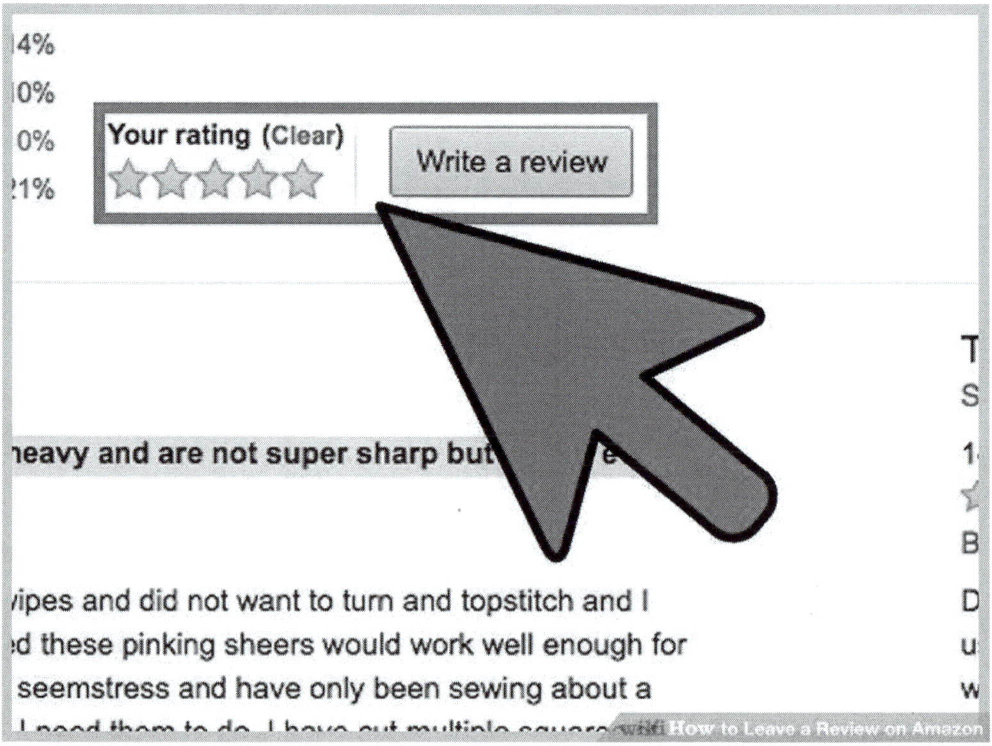

www.credibilitymethod.com/free

Let's go ahead and talk about who this book is designed for,
and then we'll get started.

THIS BOOK IS FOR YOU **IF**:

- Maybe you do not have a mentor or someone to hold your hand...

- Maybe you do not have a huge budget to pay your way to superstardom and high authority...

- Maybe you're not a public speaker or experienced presenter...

- Maybe you don't have connections to get featured in magazines or podcasts...

- Maybe you still have a full time job but would rather be a full time authority in your niche...

- Maybe you don't have thousands of followers and fans online....

- Maybe you're not getting the engagement online that you know you should be...

- Maybe you have something great to share, but nobody seems to listen...

OR... Maybe you're already on your way to crushing it, and you just picked up this book to see if you could learn anything new. This is for you as well, and you most definitely will. I guarantee it.

INTRO

6:30am - The bright sun beams through the windows of my master bedroom and strikes me in the face. I kiss Brooke goodbye, tell her she looks amazing, and wish her a great day as she leaves for work.

7am - I'm up and need a glass of water and an espresso before walking out onto the balcony and clearing my head for the day before I begin checking my emails (I usually don't eat breakfast). Some of my clients spend thousands in advertising overnight, so I religiously check in the morning for any important notifications that might need handling.

7:30am - I listen to an uplifting podcast or read a couple chapters of a book since I can spare the half hour. Sometimes I listen to music because it constantly inspires me and puts me on the right vibe.

8am - My buddy Jordan calls me and tells me about the new GM gig he snagged at a very popular local bar, and says they need marketing help asap. I set a meeting for 3pm this afternoon.

8:30am - Shower and get ready for the day. Always dress to impress. The way you see yourself is the way everyone sees you.

9am - Arrive at the office. I bring a big tray of veggies for everyone because I'm legit. I check my emails once again before getting down to work. An old friend Christian reaches out to me and says we need to chat. He wants to offer me equity in a large startup he's a part of in exchange for an advisory seat on the board. I let him know I'm interested and that we need to set up a call.

9:30am - While I arrange the task board and wait for everyone to arrive at the office, I quickly scroll through Instagram. I've gotten a handful of direct messages since yesterday, one which is an invite to appear on a new podcast that has just launched and expects to have a large audience, I accept.

10am - Staff arrives. We meet and arrange the task board for the day and get to work. Some of our clients spend up to a quarter million per month in advertising.

11am - My good friend Chris calls me out of the blue from Siesta Key Beach and asks me if I'd like to be one of the key speakers at the next conference in Miami with Grant Cardone. I accept, ofcourse.

11:30am - A client of mine, Mike, texts me to let me know that he's just brokered a deal on a new Lexus for a client of his and that he will be sending me a commission on PayPal shortly. My company handles Mike's advertisements and we generate about 40 leads per day for his auto brokerage. Everytime he closes a deal, I get paid.

12pm - I walk over to the cafe for a cappuccino and some lunch. An influencer and friend of mine, Casey, calls me saying that he needs a photographer ASAP to take some candid shots during his video shoot for K Swiss and Gary Vaynerchuk's new sneaker launch. I make a couple calls and deliver the favor within the hour. He ultimately returns the favor by connecting me with Nicole, who has a following of over 200k and is launching a new luxury sunglasses brand this summer. My company will now be building the brand's website. Her sunglasses sell for $1,000 or more.

1pm - Quick meeting with a real estate client of mine. She stops by to go over her reports that we provided the month prior, and to game plan for the upcoming month. We chat about increasing her budgets, and about some new creative assets for her advertising campaigns. She also mentions that her husband says "thank you" for the referral I sent over to his 3D rendering company. My referral turned into a great client for them. I put that favor 'in the bank' to cash in at a later date.

2pm - I have a scheduled call with my good friend Skylar. I met him a while back and saw a lot of potential in him and he reminds me a bit of myself. I've made a point to stay in touch with him over the past couple of years because I know he will do big things. During our call, he mentions that he runs a lot of money through his company credit line for his social media agency. I recommend that he uses a particular credit card to do so – the Chase Ink Business Preferred, because he will get 3X points on advertising spend. I tell him that he needs to apply and that I will send over my referral URL for him to use. He accepts. Him accepting the referral earns me 50,000 Ultimate Rewards points. I will use those points to fly my team out to Dallas free of charge in October for an event I'm speaking at with Ryan Stewman, another client of mine. He's known as the

'Hardcore Closer' – one of the top sales trainers in the world, and I'm honored to call him a friend.

3pm - I send my right hand man, my best friend and brother Matt, over to the office of one of our clients. The client is a local plastic surgeon and we are working on improving his lead generation process. Matt is spending the day there to watch and observe how the front desk staff operates, answers the phones, and closes deals. Being able to see exactly what happens after we generate a lead for a client helps us understand the bottlenecks in the business, and helps us adjust our overall strategy.

4pm - I head over to a local tech consulting firm called Impact Makers for their quarterly social. My friend Frank invites me each quarter. Frank is a commercial realtor and master of building relationships. The social event is focused on a particular type of business called a B Corporation. "B Corps" are basically businesses who commit to giving a percentage of their bottom line net profit to a dedicated non profit organization each quarter. These types of businesses have a lot of pull in the community because of the brownie points they earn by supporting a good cause. Frank is about fifty years of age and he invites me to these events because he knows I'm a young power player here. I also think he wants me to turn my agency into a B Corp, which I've considered. B Corps can receive large grants from the community that can be used to grow the business and implement the power of good. The more money you make, the more you would donate to the non-profit, therefore the grant money is usually free.

6pm - Speaking of non-profits, I am a board member of a local 501C3 that supports bicycle safety in my city and donates funds to children with traumatic brain injuries and other important causes. We have a meeting on the first Monday of each month at 6pm. I use the tools and resources that we have access to within my agency to boost the non-profit's marketing efforts. My company also built the non-profit a free website which would usually come with a five thousand dollar price tag. Being part of a non-profit comes with a lot of perks and powerful networking opportunities. My agency knows it's way around Google quite well, so we applied for a free grant which gives the non-profit ten thousand dollars per month in free Google advertising. Needless to say, the board now speaks very highly of me and they have become great friends of mine.

6:30pm - The meeting ends, and my team and I head over to the City Stadium to see the 'Kickers' game. They are the city's soccer team and also a client of mine. Brooke meets me there. We catch most of their games and enjoy free box seats with the official dental provider of the soccer team, who is also our client. We eat free dinner, have a couple free beers, and have a good time. I also invited my friend Rafael and his wife so that he could enjoy the game and the view from the box. He is a private helicopter pilot and friend of mine. He provides very powerful people with transportation to D.C. which is 2 hours north by car, 18 minutes by helicopter. I know that by sharing awesome experiences with him and becoming friends, he will likely do business with me.

8pm - I arrive home. It's always hard to leave this place, but it's entirely worth it once I get back from a hard day's work. Brooke

     www.credibilitymethod.com/free

and I put a lot of effort into making sure that "home" is a place that we can enjoy, be inspired by, and relax in. When I first get back, my mind is usually racing a million miles per hour because I am still in work mode. Many people want you to believe you should be hustling twenty-four-seven. That's not for me, but honestly, if you're single – go for it.

9pm - Once I've wound down a bit, I usually focus on personal stuff. I work on things such as this book you're reading right now, or my training programs, etc. During the day there is too much going on for me to be able to work on such things, so now is a good time to knock out an hour or so of my personal work. However, during the evening I get a lot of notifications on my phone. Everytime a client of ours gets a new lead, my phone notifies me. Many Americans are surfing the web at 9pm, and in California it is 6pm, meaning that the entire country is online. It gets wild.

10pm - Time to check the financial markets and end the night with Brooke. I utilize autotrading software that uses computer algorithms to grow my money ★. A few short years ago things were much different, Brooke worked 4 jobs so that I could become an entrepreneur. She used to show up at my house and bang on the door at noon to wake me up and remind me of my goal to one day become successful. I was a lazy bum, a clown. There's not a single day that goes by that I don't think about how important she is to me. The least I can do is forget about work for an hour and spend time with her. During the weekends we spend a lot more time together and usually go out to dinner.

11pm - As I'm brushing my teeth and getting ready to call it a night, I get an Instagram DM – *"Hey man, how much does it cost to get on a 30 minute call with you? I need some business advice and I know you're the best out there."* So, I set a reminder in my phone to answer in the morning and set up the call for my usual hourly rate.

IN THIS BOOK...

Is to show you the exact process I followed to become a superstar in my industry, grow my impact, and become a go-to resource for big businesses, influencers, and celebrities. **It's called the T.R.E.K. Method and we will cover it in this book.**

PRECURSOR

These things don't happen by chance. I've designed my life in a methodical manner and opportunities are constantly presented to me.

Keep in mind, that not every single day is like this. The more money you make, the more free shit you will get. The more connections you'll have, the more people will throw opportunities and resources at you, and around and around we go.

Now look, things were obviously not always like this. I started pursuing success at the age of 24 as kind of a dipshit to be honest. I am not college educated, I was not born with money, and my parents are not entrepreneurs. I'm covered in tattoos including my hands, have a beard, and I've been told I have a 'resting bitch face' (which i'm pretty sure is true). If I can figure out how to demand respect, become an authority in my niche, and become a highly paid consultant, you can too.

Imagine a life full of power, respect, opportunities, and abundance. *You deserve all of it.* Whether you're in a full time career, working a part time job, self employed, or a full blown entrepreneur - you need to increase your credibility if you want to continue moving upward and onward at a fast pace.

     www.credibilitymethod.com/free

WHAT MAKES THIS DIFFERENT?

You might be wondering what makes this book different than many other books you may have read before. I have a real business. My goal is not to be your favorite guru. My career is not made off of teaching you how to do this. However, I have consistently climbed the ladder higher than people I once looked up to, and I am willing to show you how I've done it. Whether you apply this information or not is up to you.

I have worked with people such as James Arthur (3x Platinum Best New Artist - American Music Awards), Aaron Carter (3x Platinum Artist and Singer), Sam Singleton (Award Winning Vocalist & Artist), Adam Wenig (Clickfunnels 2 Comma Club Member), Theresa Depasquale (WBFF Pro & Nationally Recognized Fitness Expert), Ryan Stewman (Multi-Millionaire Sales Trainer), Casey Adams (17 year old author & influencer), and many more.

I've also worked with internationally recognized brands such as Remax, Long and Foster, iHeart Radio, and more. I have been featured in Marketwatch, Yahoo Finance, The Wall Street

Journal, CBS, ABC, NBC, Fox News, Washington Business Journal, The CW, and many others for my accomplishments in the digital marketing industry.

So, I've obviously done a lot of things right. I've also done quite a few things very wrong. At 21, before I became an entrepreneur, I was a complete idiot. When I first discovered entrepreneurship at 24 and tried spreading positivity and trying to share opportunities – I was met with a disappointing result at best. I used to get hung up on daily, ignored, ditched, and disrespected. People thought I was a joke. *"How could Myke ever succeed?"*

After doing this for over 5 years now, here is what I have discovered:

- People do not want to work with you if you are not exclusive.
- Opinions of you are created within 1/24th of a second.
- Your mental and physical 'posture' determine your level of authority.
- Knowledge and leverage are your two most valuable assets in business.

I found all of these things out the hard way. This book will walk you through the easy way, and you can read the entire thing in just a couple of hours or less.

Here's the hard way:

- Spending a ton of money on self-promotion methods that don't work.
- Trying to message friends and random strangers on social media about your products or services.
- Trying to "find" and hunt down new customers for your product or company.
- Blending in with everyone else in the industry because they're all doing the same thing.

Here's the easy way:

- Having access to the best self-promotion tools in the world for cheap or even free.
- Your friends and partners constantly refer new business, customers, and clients to you.
- New customers are constantly searching for you online, and new people are discovering you everyday.
- You stand out in your industry because you have authority and people know you're the best.

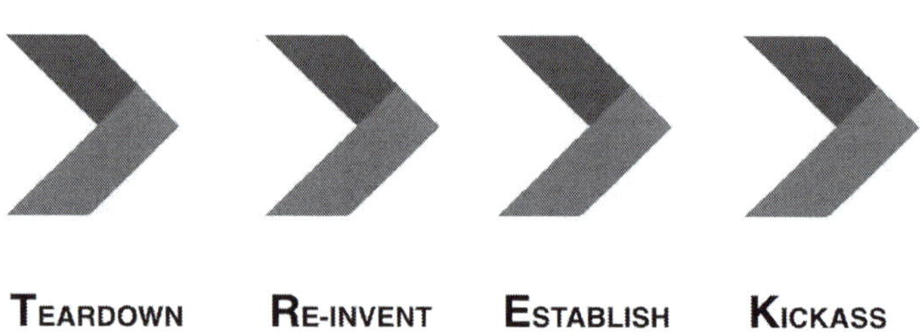

TREK: *verb* \ *trek - A long arduous or complex journey involving difficulty or hardship.*

Following the T.R.E.K. Method™ will help shorten and simplify your journey. This method is broken down into four sections within the rest of this book. Each step is numbered one through four, and within each section are mini chapters that cover the related principles. I encourage you to mark each section for you to relate back to later, and to highlight the lessons that stand out to you within each step.

My promise is to show you the exact process I followed to become a superstar in my industry, grow my impact, and become a go-to resource for big businesses, influencers, and celebrities. It's called the T.R.E.K. Method™ and we will cover it in depth within this book.

1. TEARDOWN

I have used this process repeatedly throughout the past several years to help me achieve success. Before the pivot point happened, I had to tear down and tear away everything and everyone I knew. The teardown is absolutely the hardest phase. You'll have to truly dig deep and push through this process because for many of my readers this could mean cutting off some of your family members and even your best friends in certain situations.

The best way that I can relate to you is by sharing my experience of getting rid of my friends. I had a handful of very close "friends" when I was a teenager and throughout my early twenties. These are people that I no longer speak to.

THE PIVOT

Now, maybe you're thinking that this part of the book might not relate to you, but I'm going to insist that you do not skip it. If you're reading this right now and you are currently not where you want to be in life, that is a direct reflection of your surroundings – including your friends. In order to begin re-inventing yourself, you cannot bring along any anchors or distractions.

My two biggest anchors were my friends and the people I spent my time with, and lying. Fortunately, lying was a simple one to resolve and move past. Before the pivot point, I truly did not know that I could be happy and successful. Once I learned new principles such as the law of attraction and the power of positive thinking, my thought process drastically changed. I used to lie about things because I was unhappy, and I had a made up image in my mind of what I thought people wanted to see and hear. I would lie about stupid things, such as going to college. I actually used to tell people that I was college educated because I thought it somehow meant that I was smarter and more accomplished. I later learned that this couldn't be further from the truth.

I'm not sure at what point during childhood I picked up the habit of lying or why. All I know is that I lied about things because I was unhappy with myself and my surroundings. So, I let my mind make up a different story and I chose to try and believe it. By telling other people those stories, it helped me convince myself that my actual reality wasn't true.

     www.credibilitymethod.com/free

I was born with an extremely rare skin condition known as epidermolysis bullosa simplex. It affects less than one in one hundred thousand people and causes the skin to be very fragile. It affected me quite a bit when I was young, but not so much anymore. Regardless, I also used to lie about this. The condition left me with some serious scarring on my legs and I was embarrassed about it, so I made up a story about being in a motorcycle accident. Now, I actually have been in a motorcycle accident, however, my scars were not caused by that. Maybe this was a decent excuse for lying, but I still personally have come to believe that it's unacceptable. I've also learned that by sharing the truth and embracing the things you are embarrassed about, you will actually earn the trust and respect of others. Everybody has flaws and if you openly embrace and share them, you will live a more rewardable and carefree life.

Think about how this applies to your life or career. You may not be the best or have the most talent in your industry, but if you can own up to that and accept it, it will allow you to move forward faster. In my industry, many people stretch the truth about the income they earn and about the success they've had. My opinion is that most people are not stupid, and the majority of people are also skeptical of these young 'digital marketers' or whatever they'd like to call themselves. I usually lean towards thinking that these "entrepreneurs" on Instagram are usually full of shit. Unfortunately, when I meet a lot of them my suspicions are confirmed. However, when I see people who are sharing their hustle and being open about their struggles, I am much more likely to endorse that person and try to pay attention to their journey, like Skylar who I mentioned earlier. The *journey* is always much more fun and interesting to observe than someone who seems to be at the peak *already*.

You must take action and begin to tear down everything around you. This includes lying, hanging around the wrong people, wasting your time and energy, wasting your money, and being lazy. Becoming successful is not easy, and the principles you live by will determine how difficult your specific journey will be. Too many people believe in 'luck'. The only way you will become successful is by setting the goal, creating the right intentions, and taking all out massive action. If you're the type of person who sees something that needs to be done, such as cleaning the cat's litter box – but you choose to put it off, you do not have what it takes to be successful. If you are the type of person who pisses on the toilet seat and especially chooses not to clean it up, you will never become successful. Choose to tear down everything in and around you, and choose to 'cut off the fat' in your life.

At 22, I was a part-time bartender in the city of Richmond, VA (where I still live today). Now, let me first inform you that I live in a very interesting and unique place. Richmond lands at number 3 for the most tattooed city in the United States. Here's the thing though, the city I live in is only 5 miles across. It is slowly becoming one of these mini-mega cities, and more and more people come here every year. In fact, it only placed 3rd behind Las Vegas and Miami - two of the biggest and most popular cities in the world. In Richmond, anybody who works at a coffee shop, bicycle shop, bar, retail store, restaurant, or really anything other than a bank or professional establishment – is usually completely covered in tattoos. Face, neck, hands, everything.

My city is very strange in certain perspectives. For example, I am a top performing consultant for professional businesses such as real estate brokerages, financial advisors, practitioners, doctors, dentists, and more. I am in the *very last* career that anyone would expect when they first meet or see me. I literally advise millionaire business owners what to do with their advertising dollars, and my company manages it for them through their marketing. Yet somehow, nobody blinks an eye about the fact that I have tattoos on my hands and neck etc, and could quite possibly be a total degenerate (*even though I'm not, and hopefully you aren't either*). My clients happily pay for my company's help. When someone requests a meeting, they usually end up sitting with me directly, and even though I've sometimes never met these people in person, they never question anything I say, and they listen to and follow my advice. In this book, we are going to cover the reason **why** this happens. So please understand that you have no excuse as to why you cannot demand respect in your industry.

REWIND

At 22, I was flat broke and in debt for numerous reasons which I'll explain briefly in a minute. I was ending a relationship with someone who was actually engaged to another man. She lived with him in D.C., and was also pregnant with his child. Meanwhile, I was the *'boyfriend'* who had been dating her for two years, and had no clue this was going on. She had met him towards the end of our relationship, and it made me realize that I wasn't as awesome as I thought I was. I began to realize that most of the people close to me had zero respect for me, and I can't say that I blame them.

I'VE DONE A LOT OF THINGS WRONG...

I was usually drinking every day and night, even when I was at work. I had been fired from over 13 jobs prior to becoming a

 www.credibilitymethod.com/free

bartender. Bartending was the only thing that made sense for me. I thought I was cool, and I liked to party, drink, and flirt with women – so I thought it was a pretty great idea at the time.

During my 2 year stint of bartending, I was hanging out with complete idiots, putting myself into a deep financial hole, and my parents were most likely not so proud of me. I had planned on selling my car (the only thing of value I owned) and a close friend of mine at the time, TJ, ended up stealing it from me. That's a long story that we won't get into, but the point is that for some reason people felt comfortable walking all over me. In hindsight, it was completely my fault. You likely have things that may be happening in your life right now that are not ideal. I personally have decided to take responsibility for the faults and problems in my life that have occured, and I encourage you to do the same.

I haven't spoken to TJ since that happened. As a matter of fact, I don't speak to anyone from my *old* life. My original plan was to sell my car, move to the city, go to trade school, and get my life together. That didn't happen. Instead, I spent my days and nights partying, working at bars and strip clubs, surrounding myself with idiots, and investing my time,energy, and money into bad habits. I lived in a shit-hole that set me back just $100 per month in rent – the roof was caving in, the bathroom was falling through the ceiling, and the toilets as well as the appliances barely worked. The worst part is, I couldn't even afford the rent. I'd constantly hide from my landlord to avoid paying it. My bedroom was no bigger than a closet and I would even hang my clothes on the wall with thumbtacks since I had nowhere else to put them.

In early 2014, my past came to bite me in the ass, and I had to spend 4 weekends in jail for receiving my 3rd "driving on a suspended license" ticket. Before serving my time in jail, I met Brooke. She handed me a book called "The Power" and it truly changed the way I looked at life.

Those four weekends in jail are the **pivot point** that I will relate back to throughout this book. I'm not sure where I would be if that didn't happen to me. See, in jail you don't have the comforts of everyday life. You aren't eating quality food, and you're drinking tap water out of the sink. There are no televisions, games, or friends. To sum it up, you have no distractions. You are completely isolated with your own sober thoughts. This was the first time I had truly been able to reflect on my life and my current situation because I had zero influence around me. There were no friends inviting me to the bar, there were no text messages, no music, no alcohol, nothing.

I can truly pinpoint this as the best thing that could have ever happened to me back then. During my second weekend, I was able to "smuggle" the book that Brooke gave me into jail, by hiding it in a sweatshirt that the guards somehow did not check during intake. I got lucky, but I then repeated that method the following weekend and was actually able to get an iPod in with me as well. I used that iPod to listen to Eric Thomas's *The Secret to Success: When You Want to Succeed as Bad as You Want to Breathe'*.

Reading and listening to this information completely re-programmed the way that I thought. I felt that everything I

www.credibilitymethod.com/free

had learned up until this point in my life was a complete lie. Looking back, most of it definitely was in fact false. My past experiences in life caused me to be angry and mad at the world all of the time. After the pivot point, it's almost as if a switch was flipped and I could see the world from a completely different perspective. I had 'woken up' in a sense. #woke #lol

The reason I share this with you is because I want you to think about how **you** can reenact this situation. What or *who* do you need to surrender or 'give up' in order to isolate yourself from your current situation?

- A toxic relationship?
- Drugs? Smoking or drinking?
- Sleeping in late?
- Creating space between you and negative family members?
- Friends?
- Self-hate?
- Pessimism?
- Health?
- Drama?

It could be one or all of these things. Sometimes the people closest to us are the ones that make moving forward in our lives very difficult. For me, those people were my friends and my prior relationship.

CHANGING YOUR SURROUNDINGS

Many people judge your credibility and legitimateness based on you and your surroundings. Comparing a hoodrat living on couches to a well presented businessman valeting his Bentley at the Ritz opens up the realization of habits and change.

How does someone like Example 1 transform into Example 2? He must imagine it first in his mind, and begin to present himself differently. Now, this is quite the challenge, but it must be a daily habit within your life. If you want to become successful, you must present yourself as a successful person right now in the present. There are no excuses.

Even Mark Zuckerburg, although he wears a hoodie and jeans and isn't the formal businessman you would usually see on the cover of Forbes – he is well spoken, very smart, and has a very great understanding of big business. I encourage you to watch his interviews on YouTube, as well as Steve Jobs, in order to see the impact of how these people carry themselves.

I spend a lot of time focused on how I carry myself, and in return people respond to me accordingly. If you are someone who is usually slouched over and soft spoken, people will respond to you accordingly. Think about how you speak to an old lady. Imagine sitting next to a 91 year old woman with a cane standing at a bus stop, and you were to offer her your seat – you would say something like "Hi miss, would you like to have a seat?". What if she needed help with her bags? You'd say "Oh let me help you with those, I can carry them for you." You would most likely speak softly and drag out your words, much

   www.credibilitymethod.com/free

like how you speak to a baby. Now this isn't just because *only you* would do this – just about everyone does this. When you speak to your Grandma you speak to her with love, kindness, and affection.

When people look at you like a slouched over old lady who can't do a goddamn thing for yourself, and can't take action on what you need to get done, people will speak to you as if you're a little bitch.

Now I'm sure you know plenty of people like this. The guy you know who constantly takes selfies of themselves, or the guy who is constantly getting friend zoned by the women around him. The business world functions exactly the same way. When you do or say stupid shit that makes you look inexperienced, unintelligent, or incompetent – people will treat you accordingly.

The reason I know this to be true, is because of the way I carried myself leading up to the pivot point. When you don't respect yourself, you will consequently reflect that outwards. Your posture and outwards aura is much like a loudspeaker. Whatever you plug into a speaker determines the noise that comes out of it. Put great thought into what you are 'plugging in', because it is exactly what will reflect outwards. More on that later.

Changing your outwards image can be very difficult, but if you understand 'why' it is difficult, it will make this process much easier for you. So let's get a couple things straight first; If you want to become more credible and have more legitimacy in your life and career, you need to understand that in most situations your future self is going to have brand new people around you. These are people that most likely do not currently know you. If you're in a career, imagine yourself further up the ladder. I mean *so* far up that you're in a brand new circle of influence. If you're breaking into entrepreneurship for the first time, understand that your old friends will likely not be a part of your new friend group. For a while, you will likely have no friends at all. If you're going to reinvent yourself, all of this is part of the process.

ALWAYS PUT YOURSELF FIRST

The reason the current people around you may not be able to see you as a future success, is because most of them have probably known you for some time. Think about your parents, siblings, and closest friends. They already know "who you are", which makes it very difficult for them to understand the change you're trying to make or the journey you are on. What happens when you begin planning to make drastic leaps forward in your life, is that you make the people around you uncomfortable. You are now highlighting the fact that *they are not* moving forward, and even if that is not your intention, it is how those people will feel.

When you plan on getting that new promotion, or landing that big deal or making that next big sale, or starting a new company – keep in mind that most people are just *normal*. They are looking forward to the weekend or the next big game. They aren't reading books, becoming entrepreneurs, or trying to work their way up the ladder of success. So, their first reaction is to think of what you're doing as 'stupid,' because their thoughts come from a place of lack and sometimes even anger. However, they will not *tell* you that. Instead, they will insist on the opposite and tell you that they are just looking out for you and want the best for you.

Get yourself out of these types of conversations, and away from these people. It will be one of the most difficult things you will ever have to do, but it will be the most impactful breakthrough you will ever have.

As of the writing of this book, I was stuck in a late night job about 6 years ago and I was surrounding myself with people that had bad habits, did not have my best interest at heart, and were kind of pieces of shit. They held me back tremendously. You might be experiencing that exact same thing right now, and the message that I want to share with you – is that your number one priority should be yourself. Some people might say, "well, Myke, that sounds quite selfish", but here's what I'm getting at – in order for *you* to be able to move forward in your life and become successful, or travel the world, or find an amazing relationship, you have to develop *yourself* first.

People always say "it's not what you know, it's who you know", and people think that you have to know somebody famous or have some sort of powerful connections in order to make success become a reality. However, that is not the truth. Actually, it is *all* about what you know, because what you know is what will attract *who* you know. At 24 years old I had the epiphany that I needed to cut out all of the toxic people in my life.

Since I surrounded myself with people who did not have any interest in becoming a better person, I became the same way. I felt stuck in that position as a bartender. I became unhealthy from drinking myself to death, I wound up in a horrible relationship, and was consequently unsuccessful and broke. I finally decided to cut them out of my life. I've heard a lot of people say, well, Oh, you're a sellout, or "that's messed up". People would ask me "why would you do that to your friends, how could you do such a thing?" Well, here's what I've learned – there are some amazing people in your life right now, but not

     www.credibilitymethod.com/free

everybody is meant to be in your life forever. There are many things in your life that will come and go. There are experiences and things that happen in your life such as love, travel, adventures, and many other things that happen at a particular time that likely changed the trajectory of your life forever – but those people might be gone, or those things might not be happening anymore. However, they set you on a path that changed your life in a small way, or maybe in a big way. Maybe you've lost a friend or a parent. Maybe someone close to you stole from you or betrayed your trust. These things happen, but you will come out stronger because of it. The same is true about getting rid of the toxic people around you.

I changed my life in an extremely big way by cutting out shitty friends and toxic surroundings within my environment. This includes my bad habits, and I encourage you to do the same. In a world full of politics, arguments, social media, and unnecessary egos, you must force yourself to find a way to eliminate these things. It will be hard. Ignoring friends and not answering texts and phone calls when people wanted to spend time with me was something I had to do when I first decided to become an entrepreneur. I had to in order to make my dream life come to fruition. Even back then, I constantly dealt with people trying to influence me to come drink at the bar with them. They would say, "Hey Myke, you work for yourself now right? So come to the bar and just take a shot. That's why you're doing this in the first place right? Time freedom?"

In the beginning, I thought to myself, "well, yeah, that makes sense, maybe I should just have one drink or take a shot." I thought I had been working hard and that I *deserved* it, even when I hadn't truly accomplished anything.

When this happens to you, you must have the pig-headed discipline to cut off that type of "fat" in your life. It's mandatory. There is *no way* you can move forward if you're surrounding yourself with people that drag you down. You are who you surround yourself with. I was surrounding myself with people who were on drugs and getting drunk every single night. They had horrible jobs and they were miserable. They didn't make any money, other than maybe a couple hundred dollars per week, and you know what? I wasn't even at *that* level.

Wake up call! – you are where you are in your life because you've chosen to be there. I don't care what excuses you have and nobody else does either. We all have undesirable things that have happened to us. It doesn't really matter. You can choose to be a winner or you can choose to fucking whine about it like everybody else. You've got to stay focused or your mind will destroy you, and that's what happened to me. I was destroying myself from the inside out. My mental state, my physical health, my financial health, my overall well-being and more were at stake. The saddest part is that it was simply because I made the decision to hang out with people that were not moving forward themselves, and not helping me progress in my life either.

Stop watching the news. Stop paying attention to Donald, Hillary, and the politics. Turn off the TV. Don't read the newspaper. Stop looking at Kim and Kanye. Stop feeding into people's negativity and drama. Do not surround yourself with

 www.credibilitymethod.com/free

people who are broke or unhappy. Do not allow negativity into your life. There are people in third world countries that don't complain about the shit that you might be complaining or feeling down about in your life right now. They'd be grateful to have the problems that you have, and the drama that you might have, and maybe even the iPhone that you have, or the Macbook that you have, or the home that you live in, but they don't.

Your Memories on Facebook

Myke, we care about you and the memories you share here. We thought you'd like to look back on this post from 6 years ago.

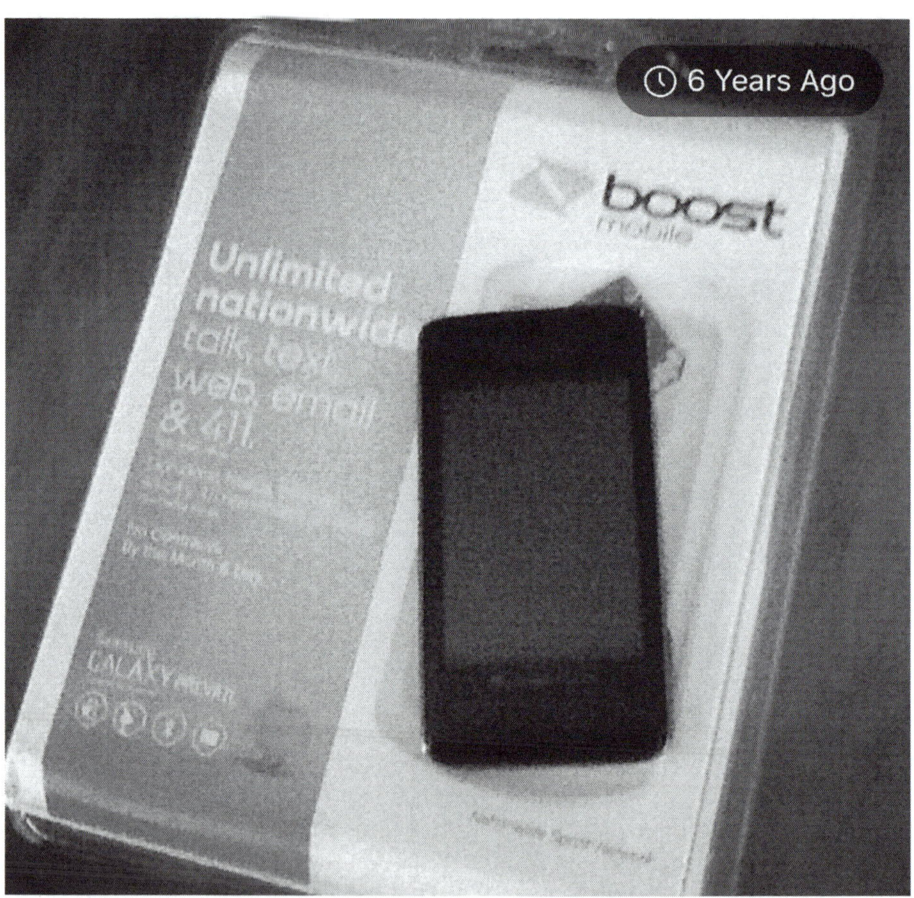

Take this for what it's worth. In 2014, I scraped off the bottom of the barrel and cut those people (*the worst people*) out of my life. I had a 'Boost Mobile' cell phone at the time and a negative balance in my bank account. See, I had never accumulated more than $400 or so in the bank until I was almost twenty five years of age. I lived in a house that was collapsing and falling apart from the inside out. The external part of my life reflected the internal quite accurately. I'm going to show you how you can change your external surroundings.

I want you to write down 3 things that you can focus on removing from your life within the next 30 days:

____

____

____

Your input equals your output. So my question for you is, what are you putting into your mind? What are you putting into your body? What are you putting into your phone? What are you putting into your bank account? What are these things that you're "plugging into" your life? You're plugging things into your life just like a speaker. Think about a speaker for a moment. You plug in something that determines the music, and what comes out is music from the speaker. If you laid an old dirty record onto a broken record player, your sound quality would be total shit. However, if you connect via bluetooth to a brand new Bose speaker with the iPhone X, you would receive a higher quality result. *You* are the speaker of your own life. What you plug into your life will determine your results. It's as simple as that.

Are you plugging things into your life that will exponentially change things in a good way? Or are you plugging in something that contributes to negativity or failure?

Here's reality: Maybe you'll die from diabetes, maybe you won't ever retire. Maybe social security will fail you. Maybe the banking system will fail you. Maybe your parents, friends, family, or your job will fail you. Maybe you'll work for 25 years for a company who doesn't give a shit about you and they flush you down the toilet like they do their other executives. You never truly know, unless you determine your own outcome. The way you determine your outcome is by choosing the things you're plugging into your life.

Here's the point: You've got to put yourself first. You must be your own priority. What I've learned from T Harv Eker is that if you help one person solve one problem, you can make a little bit of money. If you help a lot of people solve that same problem, you can make a lot of money, and if you can help a lot of people solve a lot of problems, you'll become wealthy for the rest of your life – spiritually, physically, mentally, financially, forever. However, you can't do any of this unless you're prepared to do so.

There's no way that you can help someone else's success, unless you are further along than that person. The only way that you'll get paid to help others with your product or service, is to become a credible source. If you can't make advances in your

     www.credibilitymethod.com/free

own life, no one will ever pay you. If you hang around with people that are below you, there's no way that they can lift you up either.

2. RE-INVENT

Changing your outwards image can be very difficult, but if you understand 'why' it is difficult, it will make this process much easier for you. When you don't respect yourself, you will consequently reflect that outwards. Your posture and outwards aura is much like a loudspeaker. Whatever you plug into a speaker determines the noise that comes out of it. Put great thought into what you are 'plugging in', because it is exactly what will reflect outwards.

FAST FORWARD

Today, I travel the U.S. teaching the TREK Method and online marketing. I have shared the stage with some of the most amazing business moguls and entrepreneurs on earth, I have taught thousands of entrepreneurs how to market their business, and I have rid myself of any financial restraints.

2015 was the first year I accomplished earning $10k in a single month, which was a huge landmark for me. Some of the people whom I looked up to and watched YouTube videos of in 2014, became people that I work hand-in-hand with today.

I have a wonderful support system built around me filled with great people. I went from a drunk idiot with ZERO credibility, and being hung up on, and ignored daily when trying to pursue

 www.credibilitymethod.com/free

business of any kind… to being messaged **daily** for help and advice, being paid over $350 per hour at the current writing of this book, and receiving invitations to speak with some of the most powerful people in my industry.

Now, I didn't just 'skyrocket' to success. Gaining credibility and becoming a trusted authority in any industry or career takes time. I have sold everything from energy drinks and coupon books, to high end electronics and $8,000 water filters. I earned my first six figures by spending over 11 hours per day at home on the phone. I'm not one of those phonies that talks about sales numbers or revenue as "how much I made". When I say I made six figures, I'm talking about real money that I deposited in the bank. All because I learned the valuable skill of organizing leads and constantly following up. I had the pig headed discipline to follow up with certain leads sometimes over a year at a time until they purchased. In some cases, my commissions were over $8,000. I have experienced and learned a lot in my short 5 year career, and I have written this book because I truly believe that If you follow this information and apply what you learn, you can shortcut the process.

I will always remember where I started. I will always remember my haters and the people who have royally screwed me. However, I will forever be grateful for it all, because it has allowed me to gain an understanding of what not to do, and share with you what I have learned.

THE MCDONALDS RULE

Why don't you currently work at McDonalds?

Give that question some thought for a moment. Maybe you've worked there at some other point in your life, but the statistical probability of you having a job at McDonalds and also reading this book is very slim.

I've asked this question to my audience at dozens of seminars, and I always receive interesting answers – and most of those answers are *not* wrong.

I'll receive answers such as "the pay is too shitty", or "the food sucks". Some people may say that they "don't want to work terrible hours" or "deal with customers".

However, the answers I hear are not usually the *one answer* I am looking for. Which is that *"anyone can do it."* Think about it. Just about *anyone* can land a job at a fast food restaurant. I'd be willing to bet that if a homeless person in my city really tried to clean up a bit, put together a decent resume, and work hard to make a good first impression – they could likely land a job at McDonalds.

The reality is, that there are no real requirements for somebody to find employment at fast food chains. They do not need to be a high school or college graduate, and they do not need to have prior work experience or exceptional customer service skills.

 www.credibilitymethod.com/free

The point I'm getting at, is that I want you to ask yourself this question – "does just *anybody* in the world have access to me at anytime?"

Here's the thing about exclusivity, it demands respect and professionalism from the people around you. Are you treating yourself and your business like a McDonalds drive through? See, that's what I used to do. I used to let people come into my life, take what they want, and leave, without them handing over much in return. This happened because of the way I viewed myself, and also because I simply had zero credibility.

When you can establish yourself as exclusive, and show people that working with you is a valuable experience that not many people are qualified to have – your world will change drastically.

In the coming chapters we will talk about some strategies, tactics, and tools that you can implement immediately that will get you one step closer to becoming a credible force in your industry or career.

GAINING THE EDGE

Some may think making sales and running a business is all about 'hunting' and finding new customers. The truth is, that the experts design their lives and their professions so that their customers and clients come to them.

True power and leverage is finding a way to dominate your niche, and to do it in a sophisticated manner.

Let me explain... Here's an example:

You're not feeling so hot and decide to visit your doctor. The doctor sits you down and asks you a few questions. Some of them don't even seem related to how you're feeling, but you answer every question anyway.

Why is that? Well...

- You're in pain and you view your doctor as an expert at pain relief.
- You know your answers are an important step toward your doctor finding a remedy.
- You trust your doctor, maybe for literally no other reason than he looks and talks like a doctor.

The two of you are in rapport (a harmonious relationship based on good communication and authority).

How would you have felt if a doctor chased you down and told you all about himself, but asked no questions, gave you a

 www.credibilitymethod.com/free

packet of Tylenol® and told you to go home and rest? A little disappointed? A little cheated?

That's how your potential customers and clients feel when you don't find a way to gather intelligence about their pain or their problems. Actually, it's much worse. They view you as a novice and not an expert in your field, and nobody wants to do business with a novice.

In order for you to gain the edge, you need to 'act as if'. Now, don't confuse this with being fake. Keep in mind that this book is all about how you can be authentic while also establishing real credibility. When you are honest and open with people, they will begin to trust you.

When you're trying to gather intel about the people you'd ultimately like to sell to or offer your service to, make sure that they know you are coming from a place of honesty and straightforwardness. If you are not upfront with your customers and real with them, they will sniff it out faster than you'd think.

See, back in the day old sales tactics used to work. Mainly because communication was much less frequent back then. Today, we live in a world full of social media and there are zero barriers to contacting someone. Any given day I receive at least a hundred messages via email, Instagram, Facebook, etc. I can easily spot each and every person who is trying to sell me something or get something from me, and chances are that you can as well. Especially LinkedIn, I swear that every message I receive is some sort of weird automated bullshit.

Anyway - So remember, when you don't find a way to gather intelligence about your customer or client's pain or their problems they will view you as a novice and not an expert in your field, and nobody wants to do business with a novice.

Now, when I say "act as if", I want you to present yourself the way that you should already see yourself. For example, champion athletes likely already viewed themselves as the champion far before it actually happened. You have to carry yourself in a way that means business, professionalism, and experience. You must see yourself as the champion of your industry, and make the decision that you want to be world class.

www.credibilitymethod.com/free

A GOOD OLD FASHIONED OPINION

In this part of the book, we are going to begin shifting the focus away from me, and more towards you and the tools you're going to need. One of the most difficult parts about becoming credible, or establishing yourself as an expert, is figuring out what your advantages are. Ofcourse, you can just assume what you are good at and which things stand out about you – but it's much easier and more effective to simply ask the people who know and support you already. For example, the way I discovered that I look like an asshole most of the time, is because a friend was honest with me and told me that I am not easily approachable. This type of information is extremely helpful in business. It allowed me to become aware of my presence when meeting new people, and to make being nice a priority.

When you see a new product advertised, whether it be for a new shampoo or a new vehicle, the opinions you will value the most about certain products will be what your friends, family, associates, or even strangers who have tried the product have to say about it.

You will put a lot more weight on the opinions of friends, family, and partners about the value of a product, than you would on the producer of the advertising campaigns.

When you see an advertisement on Instagram that features Kylie Jenner holding a 'Hi Smile' teeth whitener, you think to yourself, "Yeah, riiiiiight! And just *how* much did you get paid for typing that caption?"

On the other hand, when your best friend says that he or she tried the product and it delivers everything that is promised, you would likely consider buying the product. That is the 'word-of-mouth' effect.

In the world of business and entrepreneurship, the best and easiest way to achieve the word-of-mouth effect is to simply ask your friends, co-workers, or customers what they think.

In order to get responses you may need to offer a free gift in exchange for replies but it will be worth the effort. Five dollar Starbucks gift cards are perfect. When you get positive responses about you or your brand, you'll have testimonials to post on your new website and in your press kit ★. Enthusiastic personal testimonials are one of the best ways to achieve more credibility for yourself.

YOU ARE YOUR BRAND

Branding yourself and/or your product is one of the most important aspects of gaining credibility. Branding isn't just important - it is vital and urgent. Here's 3 very simple steps to get started:

- Go to Fiverr and pay $5.00 for someone to design a simple logo for you or your brand.

- Take your logo and create a great Facebook cover photo for free with Pagemodo or Canva.

- Download 'WordSwag' for iOS or 'Fonto' for Android and create your own image quotes for your Instagram or Facebook page and share them weekly.

Branding can be done in many ways. One such way is the use of a logo. Think about the products that you buy and use every day in your everyday life. You would easily recognize many products by their logo alone even if the name of the product wasn't visible.

You can also make yourself a logo that can be included on your website, press kit, and on all of your marketing materials and correspondence using a tool like canva.com for free ★. When your logo has been seen often by enough people, you will have associated the logo with your social channels and products.

Another way to brand yourself is by using a specific term on your website and on all of your marketing materials and correspondence. For example, one of my first successful info products was called Freebie Hacks - and my students referred to themselves as freebie hackers. It helped people feel like they were a part of something, almost like a cult – but not as strange. I created a private Facebook group for the students, and branded the group as Freebie Hackers. I created a logo for the brand and even gave away free tee shirts to the students so they could rep the brand. People loved it and constantly bragged on social media about being a Freebie Hacker, which led more customers my way.

Using your name as part of your website domain and including it in the names of all of your informational products and in the headings of all of your correspondence is a simple, inexpensive and effective way of branding yourself. "Jane Doe's Secrets to Quick Weight Loss" is a simple method of branding that is effective and fairly easy to accomplish.

Branding is a broad but important topic. It's a vital step to gaining more credibility for yourself. Even incorporating branding into your resume is an excellent idea.

 www.credibilitymethod.com/free

POSITIONING

Positioning is like story telling. Done well, it can maximize your impact. Done poorly, and you'll vanish. Positioning is the most important aspect of your marketing because it lays the foundation for everything you do. Effectively done, it quickly tells the recipient of your marketing message why they should care about your product, solution, technology, or company. You can position yourself as an expert with simple tools, such as having a professional website. (★ I've provided you with your own brand new website here for free.) If you don't have a website, who in the hell is going to take you seriously anyway?

 Some other helpful hints, are to go out there and find a photographer who can take photos of you in action, or in a professional business setting. This will drastically change someone's first impression of you. A lot of high school and even college photography students will do this for free. You can use these photos in your email signature, on your website, or in your media kit.

The human brain automatically creates a judgement/opinion of what you're looking at within 1/24th of a second. It could be a person, an article of clothing, a car, or even food - an opinion is instinctually created within the brain, and the same goes for when people look at *you*.

If you're a man, get a suit or atleast a sport coat. 'Topman' is a great and affordable brand that I highly recommend. Be sure to ★ snag some business cards for cheap (I've provided you with a free design here) and be sure to include your new website domain as well as your official title if you have one. Your target audience will listen when you speak their language by emphasizing that you can use your talents to solve their problems. However, they won't listen if you sound just like everyone else in your market.

3. ESTABLISH

Positioning is like storytelling, and by telling your story well, you can establish yourself in your industry. Positioning is the most important aspect of your career because it lays the foundation for everything you do. Effectively done, it quickly tells the recipient of your marketing message why they should care about your product, solution, technology, or company. You can position yourself as an expert with simple tools, such as the website and business card.

SOCIAL PROOF

A great way to build social proof for yourself or your business is also by taking advantage of photographs, but instead this time, we're going to make sure it's by using third party credibility.

 Any time you find yourself within the radius of someone more successful than you, or a higher authority in your field, find an excuse to take a photo with this person. Then, add it to your website that you built from the positioning segment of this book.

(Marcus Lemonis, billionaire business mogul and investor from "The Profit" on CNBC)

When you attend seminars or training events for your company, be sure to get out of your comfort zone and take photographs with all of the top leaders and executives there. It's is a key

     www.credibilitymethod.com/free

factor of importance in your appearance, and the impression you create with others.

You should never, ever pass up the opportunity to attend a seminar that is even loosely based on your niche or industry. Everybody who is *'somebody'* in your chosen niche market will be at most related seminars, and you want to be one of them.

Simply attending seminars that are related to your niche market will increase your visibility. You are who you surround yourself, and if you can get close to the speakers and VIP attendees of different events, you're likely to find yourself within their circle one day. This has happened to me on multiple occasions. One of my very great friends Adam Wenig, a 24 year old millionaire, was once somebody that I watched on stage and had never met. My client Ryan, a published author and multi-millionaire, was once a keynote speaker at an event I sat front row for before we had ever met. With increased visibility comes increased credibility and that is one of your main objectives when you attend any event or seminar. If you bump shoulders with the right people, you could be introduced to the top veterans in your chosen niche market and hopefully invited to speak one day as well.

You should attend all of the lectures and discussion groups that you can possibly squeeze into the allotted time frame. Be certain that you are prepared to ask intelligent questions and listen carefully to the answers that you are given. Stay as visible as you can throughout the two or three days that the seminar lasts. By the way, dress sharp. Don't be an idiot. Well known speakers and industry veterans always look their best, so you should as well.

Do your best to get a photo with the important speakers and people at the event. You can even follow up with those people after the event by finding their email with a tool like www.hunter.io – then introduce yourself, mention the event you attended and include the photo you took with them as an attachment, and ask if there is anything you could do to assist them or their business. If you don't ask, the answer is always going to be no.

Another great way to build credibility is by landing interviews with podcast channels or local TV stations that relate to your niche.

Position yourself in front of thousands and get your story and your knowledge out there! Many podcasters are usually just trying to get interviews under their belt and find success just as you are. Hence why I've already compiled a ★ list of podcasts here for you to apply to. I've also provided you with ★ free email templates and a press kit for you to use. It's a win-win situation and it's a great way to get your name out there and build credibility. Go sign up for some free interviews today, and thank me later.

 www.credibilitymethod.com/free

LEVERAGE

In order to gain leverage on your industry and the people within it, you have to be willing to work for free, and do a lot of favors.

Why do you think I spend hours writing up books like this one in order to help you for free? It's because I want to build leverage with you so that you purchase my programs and attend my events.

The more "favor tokens" you can build with individuals, the more leverage you will gain with others when you need something. It could be a simple favor such as asking them to check out your webpage or your resume, or even meeting with you for coffee when you're in their local area.

Or maybe you're running a Kickstarter campaign and you now have the leverage to ask them if they would mind supporting you by throwing in a few bucks. You get the idea.

Work for free, and do what you have to do, until you can do whatever you want to do. On the next page, I'll give you some great ideas of how to build leverage with your potential partners and customers.

LEVERAGE IDEAS

- Article Sharing - Share a heartfelt blog post or article that relates to your prospect that they would find value in. Let them know you were thinking about them.

- Magazine Subscription - Think about what your prospect or potential client enjoys. For example; Hunting & Fishing - if you have their address, surprise them by subscribing them to a year's worth of a magazine that you feel they would enjoy. This is a great way to stay at the top of your client's mind every single month and it will only cost you a few dollars.

- Free Book - Same idea. Think about a book your client might enjoy. Mail it to them with a hand written letter wishing them a productive week etc.

- Gift Card - Send your prospect a gift card with a handwritten letter. If you do not have their address, most big brands offer options to email an e-gift card. ☆ Here's how to get gift cards for free.

- New Introduction - If you know your potential client's needs, be sure to introduce them to people that may be able to help them even better than yourself. When you help people, and humble yourself to stay out of the picture at times, you will build leverage. Your future client will feel

　　www.credibilitymethod.com/free

that they "owe you one". Trust me, it works *(refer to 1pm in the Intro section of this book).*

- Podcasting - Use the tool we talked about in the positioning segment, and when you find an interview opportunity that does not relate to you, but maybe relates to your prospective client or an influencer or mentor figure you follow, be sure to send them a personal email or direct message with the link to the interview channel or application. Let them know you thought of them, and that the interview opportunity could be a great fit for their brand. What an amazing gift to hand someone… free publicity!

- Survey - If you have addresses, put five bucks with a nicely typed questionnaire in an envelope, along with a handwritten letter. Let your prospect know that their feedback matters to you, and you're always wanting to improve your efforts. Note that you've included $5 in exchange for their honest feedback. Make sure your questions are designed to help your business. This way even if they do not hire you or purchase from you, they will always remember you and you'll also get some useful feedback to improve your business.

ANSWER THE MOST QUESTIONS

Forums are one of the most popular types of sites on the Internet today. The reason is simple; It is a place where people have the freedom to express their opinions and communicate with other people around the world about almost any topic imaginable.

Forums are places on the Internet where people with similar interests or common problems gather. You can find forums for almost any subject by using your favorite search engine, typing in keywords followed by the word 'forums' and get lots of hits.

There are forums dedicated to topics like travel, scuba diving, fly fishing, crafting, cars, and more. There are forums dedicated to topics like cancer, diabetes, and many other health conditions. There are forums dedicated to hair loss, weight control and depression. You name it - you can most likely find a forum where those who are interested in or concerned with the topic gather.

The one free forum I do recommend signing up for is called Quora. It is the biggest database of questions and answers in the world. By finding and posting to threads and questions that are related to your niche or sub niche market, you have a pool of potential customers, clients, or referrals to talk to about your industry, product, or service. There should be plenty for you to share that can help them with their problems, questions, or interests.

 www.credibilitymethod.com/free

You must not, however, go into a forum doing nothing but advertising yourself, your website or your products. Just like with anything online, you must provide some type of value first. Quora is a massive website, but there is a tight knit community within, so be patient and play it smart. Some people's answers receive hundreds of thousands of views and 'upvotes', so pay attention to how those authors answer questions and provide value to the other readers on Quora.

You must establish yourself as a welcomed contributor. After your answers and content begins to receive some views and upvotes, you can share your expertise on the subject and be seen as a friend helping a friend rather than a spammer trying to sell some shit.

WRITING YOUR FIRST REPORT OR E-BOOK

Your credibility that you will build by writing your own free report or book to be given away or distributed on your website can be an invaluable asset.

A free report on your industry or subject can be written and offered on your site in the next twelve hours or less. Now most of my readers won't do this regardless of how easy it is. You hopefully already know a bit about your subject matter, so that helps eliminate a few hours of research that would usually be necessary if you were writing on a topic that you knew nothing about.

A report of ten or twelve pages is all you will need. ★ I've even provided you with a bunch of different eBook templates for free here.

Here are some tips for creating your free report:

1. It is vital that you give your report an attention-grabbing headline.

2. You want to 'soft teach'. Be certain that your report contains quality information, but not too much vital and timely information.

3. Use bold type for sub-titles and make your point in one paragraph – never more than two paragraphs.

     www.credibilitymethod.com/free

4. Include your links or affiliate links to products that will
    provide more in depth information on subject matter
    included in the report.

5. Include links to the websites of your potential joint-venture
    partners and be sure to send a copy of the report to them
    to let them know you've mentioned them in your report.
    This will help get you on their radar.

THE CREDI-BULLET

Every product that you put out there should serve as a vehicle to build your credibility further.

Let's say that you have used the free eBook templates I've given you to write a killer eBook about how to re-style old outdated clothing into modern and up to date styles. That's information that many people would be interested in. However, if the name of the eBook is "*A Guide to Re-Styling Old Clothes*" it might make you a few dollars, but it isn't going to increase your authority or credibility in the fashion niche. You would have wasted a golden opportunity to build your credibility just by wrongly naming your product.

More important than it being a guide to re-styling old clothes, it is *your* guide. You could name the book 'John Doe's Guide to Wearing The Most Desirable Swag and High End Fashion, Without Even Swiping Your Credit Card; and kill two birds with one stone, so to speak.

Every product that you produce should have either your logo or your name attached to it. It doesn't matter what the product is or whether you are selling it or giving it away. Your products are more than just products. They are the rocket that you use to increase your visibility as well as your credibility, and neither should ever be discounted. Both will likely have a drastic effect on your bottom line.

Another important way to make the most of every info product that you produce is to insert your URL onto the cover of your product, as well as to every page either in the header or footer, just like I have done in this book.

In many ways you will make your own opportunities. You will create your own websites or have others create them for you using your ideas.

You get to pick and choose what and how you will market your own ideas, talents, and abilities. When we're busy, the one thing that we sometimes forget to do is to market ourselves. It's all about selling – and selling means selling the fact that you are a credible source of information. If you lack confidence or are afraid to sell, then I would suggest a career change.

Now I know many of my readers are in the marketing industry or aspiring digital marketers, but let's get one thing straight; starting out as a marketer is not an easy thing to do. You might set up a website and offer your digital or informational products for sale, but you are just one grain of sand on a very large beach.

I'd like to tell you that credibility can't be bought, but that simply wouldn't be the truth either. The fact is that if you have enough money almost anything can be bought, including credibility. There are plenty of idiots using paid advertising to convince the world that they're an expert even when they're not.

The Internet is a massive place, and there are millions of websites. You can use the strategies taught in this book to grow yourself into a force to be reckoned with.

4. KICKASS

You have to choose how you will market your own ideas, talents, and abilities. When we're busy, the one thing that we sometimes forget to do is to market ourselves. It's all about selling – and selling means selling the fact that you are a credible source of information. If you don't have the tools to market yourself properly, you're in for an uphill battle. In order to kickass in your industry, you have to double down on what works and always stay at the front.

CHOOSE YOUR FIGHTS WISELY

When you pick a fight you should at least have a decent chance of winning. When you first start out in any industry, it is better to choose a niche to fight in rather than a broad and competitive industry that you just might get crushed in.

For example: If you are thinking about fighting in the digital marketing provider space, you will have some heavy hitters as competition - people who have years of experience that you can't hope to compete against without deep pockets. However, if you narrow your fighting arena down to an info product about the top hacks for Wordpress ★ you won't have nearly as much competition and you will have a much better chance of success.

Another example of choosing your fight wisely for instance, is in the self-help field. You can narrow your "fight" down to one vertical such as 'anger management', which will give you a better shot at dominating that market.

No matter which niche market you are considering fighting in, you can narrow your focus down to something much more specific, thus improving your chances of gaining credibility quickly.

One real life example of narrowing a niche down to a more specific market and succeeding is that of Red Bull. Coke and Pepsi dominate the soft drink industry, however, the energy drink market didn't have much of a buzz when Red Bull first

 www.credibilitymethod.com/free

gained traction. It succeeded because it limited the competition it had to face for market share.

Choose your fights wisely. Narrow your market by choosing a sub-niche. That is a key step toward building your credibility faster.

RADIATE GREATNESS

Make the decision to implement hard work and effort into everything you do. The meaning of "kickass" in this section is to challenge you to become a producer. How can you show up and produce within every single day of your life? If you want to become world class or great at anything, it starts with building great habits and a powerful routine.

Whether it's doing the dishes, taking out the trash, or finally starting on that book you've been putting off for months - just do the work. Be willing to work harder than the next person. A short term sacrifice of time will pay off big in the long term. Set quarterly goals and measure your progress each month.

Kicking ass is synonymous with setting the right intentions and relentlessly pursuing your goals.

     www.credibilitymethod.com/free

HOW TO BUILD CREDIBILITY WITH YOUR EXPERTISE

Whether you are just starting to break into your scene, or you've been around for a while, you will likely need to begin build your own credibility alone.

This must be done before you have any hopes of getting other well known brands or influencers to joint-venture with you. A **joint venture** (JV) is a business arrangement in which two or more parties agree to pool their resources for the purpose of accomplishing a specific task. This task can be a new project or any other business activity.

Before you can begin setting up JVs with other power players, let's get you moving in the right direction first. I'm going to show you how to write articles about your niche or industry and market the articles. Your author bio at the bottom of these articles will contain your name, headshot, contact information, social media channels, and most importantly – your website address. This information will be included when another website owner or publication posts your article on their site. The benefit of this is that many of those websites already get plenty of traffic, whereas maybe yours does not yet.

To help you get a head start writing official articles for a real online publication, ★ I'm allowing my readers to become contributors on my top blog The Social Campus. Your articles will be reviewed by my team for quality and published to the blog in the order they are received.

That will get you started, but you'll want to join and actively post on other blogs and forums that relate to the subject matter of your industry. Usually you will have to apply, and now you'll have existing articles to share with the publication as examples. The tag included in your signature should have a backlink to your website. ★ I've also provided a free email template for you to use when you reach out to these websites to write for them.

Writing and marketing articles on your niche topic is one of the best, fastest, and free ways of gaining online credibility. It is also the first domino to knock over on your path to getting verified on social media one day as well.

The Internet gobbles up information at an alarming rate. The market for good articles is almost unlimited. If you can write well, this is one of the fastest ways to help build your credibility. You can write and submit articles to article banks as well. The articles will, hopefully, be picked up and republished by other website owners and publications. These articles, which contain your website address, contact, and other information, will add links for search engines to crawl and help improve your page rank (PR Score) in search results.

 www.credibilitymethod.com/free

It will also give you needed exposure in your quest for credibility and allow you to share your expertise on your niche topic or, better yet, your sub niche topic. You can then showcase these articles on your website and social media, or even email them out in a newsletter to your clients and potential customers.

The articles that you write for the purpose of gaining credibility for yourself should contain specific 'ingredients' if they are to be chosen and republished.

Ingredient #1: Your articles must have attention-grabbing titles that include the keywords for your niche market. You can use this headline tool for free: www.portent.com/tools/title-maker

Ingredient #2: Your articles must have a polarizing first sentence in the first paragraph to keep readers reading, as well as a high quality and relevant image. You can find amazing images at www.unsplash.com

Ingredient #3: Your articles must be rich with relevant keywords for your niche market.

Ingredient #4: Your articles must contain pertinent and timely information that readers will find of value. It cannot be junk, and you cannot just copy and paste something. If you do this, you will cause a duplicate content error on the owner's site – and they will be quite unhappy with you.

Ingredient #5: Your author bio needs to contain your full name, contact information, social channels, and links to your websites.

These techniques are designed to drive traffic to your website and social channels, as well as to start establishing your credibility. On your website you'll want to have something the visitor can take with the, such as your resume, portfolio, or even a free report that can be downloaded in exchange for the visitors information.

     www.credibilitymethod.com/free

ADVERTISING FOR MASSIVE EXPOSURE

It is true that paid advertising can be very expensive. It is also true that, if you are like many new entrepreneurs, money can be an obstacle. However, using paid advertising is can be the steroids to building your credibility. You are no doubt already investing a lot of your time, effort and energy into yourself, but you may want to invest some of your hard earned money as well. Money is a tool that can create even more money for you if you leverage the right tools in the right direction. Here's a clever video ad that I run to increase my page likes on Facebook:

You must have first-hand exposure in order to effectively build your online credibility and paid advertising is one of the best ways to gain that exposure. You don't have to hire my agency to handle your paid advertising needs either.

Instead, I've put together an academy called Underground Marketing Hacks ★ where I provide plenty of simple and very affordable lessons covering online marketing, advertising, and more. Inside, I provide guest interviews with some of my closest friends from my inner circle, where they unleash their six and seven figure strategies. You can check it out at www.undergroundmarketinghacks.com - **Use code FIFTY-XNDEUJFQUCJGU** for half off anything you'd like, as a sincere thank you for reading my book. Once you learn some of this stuff, you'll be able to place your own advertisements and track the results. If you can get better at marketing, it will make this entire process much easier for you.

Look, you know your own niche well. Choose platforms that will give you the best exposure to your most targeted audience. Instagram is great for ecommerce. Google is great for professional establishments such as a doctor's office or plumbing company. Place ads for a short period of time to test and track the results. Renew paid advertisements only on the platforms that are producing the most traffic or results for you. You can even just promote your Instagram profile to gain more followers if you can't think of any other ideas.

KEEPING GUARD

One dictionary defines credibility as: *"The quality, capability, or power to elicit belief."*

Credibility is an asset that must be gained foremost by words and actions. However, it certainly stands to reason that it can be lost by words and actions as well. And credibility can certainly be lost much easier than it can be gained in the first place, so you must always be on guard.

Credibility is also established by operating one's business with a strict code of ethical behavior that demands fair and equal treatment of customers, suppliers and joint-venture partners, and then following through with competent support of all products and services that are sold.

There are right ways and wrong ways to do everything. Here are some simple rules to follow:

- Post only accurate and truthful information to any blogs that you might contribute to, as well as forums like Quora. Only after you have established yourself as a contributor in good standing of the group, using a signature tag that includes your URL is fine.

- Create informational products that are filled with helpful and useful information for those who will be using it. Be certain to include your URL, name or logo in the title and on every page of the document.

Double or triple check that all links included work and that the information is accurate.

- Provide a great support system for your customers. Conduct online sessions to answer questions and provide insight on how to make the best use of your product. Keep your communication lines open between you and your customers as well as between you and those who resell your products as affiliates.

- When something goes wrong with a product that you have sold or if it doesn't deliver what you promised, take full responsibility. Acknowledge your mistakes up front as quickly as you can and do everything within your power to make it right. The only way you will retain business is when you're willing to let others feel that they are right.

www.credibilitymethod.com/free

THE LONG GAME

If you're trying to "get rich quick", the strategies in the book will never work for you. Simply because your mind is in the wrong place, and you're not willing to provide the value - but if you've made it this far, then you're obviously not an impatient "get rich quick" type of individual.

So, put in the work, put in the hours, and position yourself as an expert. Go out there and dominate. Play chess while the rest of the world plays checkers.

While everyone else is copy/pasting long messages to random strangers on Facebook and LinkedIn, you'll spend weeks building rapport and meaningful relationships. While everyone else is trying to automate communication, you're sending out gift cards and hand-written notes.

While everyone else is pretending to be a guru and lying about their income, you'll stay humble and let everyone know that maybe you aren't where you want to be yet, but that you'll never give up and that you will in fact reach your goals. More importantly, that you're connected to the *right* people who can help your end-customer, even if you cannot help them at the moment.

The truth always wins. Never lie, because people who lie do it out of fear. Stay true to your mission and give it all you've got in order to be authentic, knowledgeable, credible - and you will **always** win.

ACKNOWLEDGEMENTS

I'd like to say thank you to many different people, so forgive me if I happen to skip over anyone. You all mean the world to me and I hope that my story and my lessons inspire you as much as you've inspired me.

First, I would not be able to spend time doing what I love without my Brooke. Thank you for working as hard as you could as I struggled to get on my feet. Thank you for always pushing me to do better. Thank you for having the patience and the ability to see better times ahead. No words that I could ever write would express my gratitude and love for you. I'd like to thank my brother Matt for leaving his home in Jacksonville to come be a part of our mission here in Virginia. My day to day would not be the same without you, and I am eternally thankful for everything you assist with. Thank you to my father Ed and stepmother Dee - without your guidance I am not sure where I would have ended up. Thank you to my mother Roni and stepfather Mike - you both have showed immense support and have always been the first to offer positivity and a place to lay my head. Thank you to my grandmother Marian - you are one of my biggest inspirations and I aspire to accomplish even a fraction of what you have been able to do throughout your lifetime.

To switch gears, I'd like to say thank you to Rich Cook - you were one of the first people to see my talent. I appreciate you to the Earth's end and back for everything you did and have done for myself and Brooke. It goes without saying, you are the man. Thank you for forcing me out of my comfort zone every hour of every day.

Thank you to my great friend Adam Wenig. It's been an honor to work alongside of you and learn together. You've always been the first person to share resources, tips, strategies, and opportunity with me. Working with you helped me deposit my first $100k into the bank. When I was 24, that was a distant dream of mine, and what seemed to be a daunting task. Although I've learned that money doesn't exactly make you happy, that moment sure did. So, thank you.

Thank you to my team here at the office and remotely, without you I would still be working out of my bedroom. Your countless hours of work and effort is to be admired and I am beyond thankful for your momentum towards our goals.

Thank you to the readers - yes, you. Without the people who have followed my journey, watched me on stage, listened to me speak or watched my videos, this book would not exist. I hope this has been helpful for you and has made an impact on your level of credibility. I appreciate you.

RESOURCES

If you would like to explore any other resources of mine please checkout the following websites:

www.mykemetzger.com
www.undergroundmarketinghacks.com
www.credibilitymethod.com
www.thesocialcampus.com
www.rvasocialmarketing.com